better together*

*This book is best read together, grownup and kid.

 akidsco.com

a kids
book
about

a kids book about

PUBLIC SPEAKING

by TEDxPortland

A Kids Co.
Editor Jennifer Goldstein
Designer Gabby Nguyen
Creative Director Rick DeLucco
Studio Manager Kenya Feldes
Sales Director Melanie Wilkins
Head of Books Jennifer Goldstein
CEO and Founder Jelani Memory

DK
Editor Emma Roberts
Senior Production Editor Jennifer Murray
Senior Production Controller Louise Minihane
Senior Acquisitions Editor Katy Flint
Acquisitions Project Editor Sara Forster
Managing Art Editor Vicky Short
Publishing Director Mark Searle
DK would like to thank Natasha Devon

This American Edition, 2024
Published in the United States by DK Publishing
1745 Broadway, 20th Floor, New York, NY 10019

DK, a Division of Penguin Random House LLC
Text and design copyright ©2022 by A Kids Book About, Inc.
A Kids Book About, Kids Are Ready, and the colophon 'a' are trademarks of A Kids Book About, Inc.
The TEDxPortland logo is the property of the global TEDx Community
and the local Portland franchise of TED and is used with permission.
24 25 26 27 10 9 8 7 6 5 4 3 2 1
001-339425-July/2024

A catalog record for this book is available from the Library of Congress.
ISBN: 978-0-7440-9892-1

DK books are available at special discounts when purchased in bulk for
sales promotions, premiums, fund-raising, or educational use. For details, contact:
DK Publishing Special Markets, 1745 Broadway, 20th Floor, New York, NY 10019, or SpecialSales@dk.com

Printed and bound in China

www.dk.com
akidsco.com

This book was made with Forest
Stewardship Council™ certified
paper – one small step in DK's
commitment to a sustainable future.
Learn more at www.dk.com/uk/
information/sustainability

This book is dedicated to every thinker, doer, and creator. Don't be afraid to use your voice for good.

Speak up!

Intro
for grownups

Communication through public speaking is a learned skill that can open possibilities and growth in all of us, no matter our age.

We wanted to write this book to illustrate the basic skills associated with public speaking and the profound benefits it can offer the kids in our lives—developing leadership skills, enriching confidence, influencing the world around us, and becoming a go-to person for ideas and solutions.

Whether in our communities, at school, at the dinner table, or on a sports team, public speaking is a way to bring people together. And most importantly, with confidence in their public speaking skills, kids can feel empowered to call out issues they see and voice their opinion on how to improve them!

As you read this book with your future changemaker, emphasize that public speaking is all about sharing your knowledge about a topic with others in a compelling way which motivates everyone to move toward good and positive change.

—Cathey, Greg, Stephen, Jelani, David, and Amy

This is a book about

PUBLIC SPEAKING.

In its simplest form, public speaking is **sharing your ideas out loud to an audience.**

We believe everyone has something important to say.

That includes YOU!

We hope this book will
help you find a way to
share your ideas with others.

Let's be honest,
public speaking can be
kind of **scary** sometimes.

So many things could happen
while you're up there
in front of everyone.

You could get nervous.

Or forget what you're going to say.

And what if people judge you?

Sounds pretty awful, right?

But what if we told you public speaking could also be kind of amazing?

That it could make you feel really proud and strong?

And hey, it might even be fun too!

We also believe more
than anything else
that public speaking
can help others.

So, who are we?

Cathey, Greg, Stephen, Jelani, David, and Amy.

We are public speakers and coaches who help others **(like you)** get up in front of people to share something important.

In this book, each of us will pop in with thoughts and ideas.

We'll put them on little sticky notes so you'll know which one of us it is.

So what is public speaking really?

Public speaking is putting yourself out in front of an audience* to share your ideas, stories, and the things you know with the people there.

*An audience is just a group of people.

Public speaking can happen in your **class, community, home, or up on stage.**

One time, I spoke at a baseball stadium.

- Jelani

For example:

imagine that 1 week from today, your assignment is to talk to your whole class about the solar system.

You'll be the only one talking, and what you share needs to last at least 5 minutes.

How does that make you feel?

It might make you wake up
in the middle of the night
with your heart racing.

That's usually
me before
a big speech!
      -Jelani

It might give you butterflies
or make you feel sick
to your stomach.

It might make you worry
you'll forget what you're
supposed to say.

What you're feeling when any of those things happen is ~~fear~~.

Fear that you might mess up or that everyone will laugh at you.

But we want you
to know something.

Something **so important** we want
to make sure you really hear us...

yone fear.

Feeling fear is totally _normal_.

And did you know that our bodies feel **fear** and **excitement** in the same kind of way?

Like, our bodies can't tell the difference between the two.

For instance, your heart might beat fast and your palms might get really sweaty when people clap for you at the end of a speech—which is a really exciting thing!

But your palms might get sweaty and your heart might beat fast when you are afraid something bad will happen too.

Your body is reacting in exactly the same way to 2 entirely different emotions. So even though you may feel nervous about public speaking, **it can also be exciting**!

And here's a little something that's exciting too...

Remember what we said about helping others? Well, sharing your ideas can *inspire* other people.

Your ideas could help someone learn something new.

Your personal story could help someone else feel less alone.

Your words could lead to important change!

They can be a gift to someone.
-Greg

Because guess what?!

You have
impo

rtant
things to say!

Would you like to know
our best piece of advice
for public speaking?

Here it goes...

Just be you!

Don't try to be like everyone else.

Some kids like sports.

I love
playing
badminton!
-Jelani

Some kids like music.

I play piano!
-Amy

Some kids like juggling.

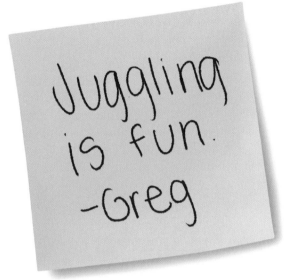

Juggling is fun.
-Greg

Some kids like being in rodeos.

I won a calf-roping event!
-Stephen

Our differences
make us **interesting**.

You've gotta just be you!

It's way better when
we aren't all the same.

And that's true
when we speak, too.

**We should feel like ourselves,
and talk like ourselves.**

And here's a little secret.

Don't worry about being perfect.

Because guess what—

you can't be!

All speakers make mistakes, even teachers and grownups.

Really great speakers learn to laugh at their mistakes instead of feeling bad about them.

When mistakes happen, shrug them off and keep going.
– Amy

So don't try to be perfect.

Practice is really what will make you feel more comfortable.

And the more you do something, the less scary it becomes.

Making your practice **playful** helps a lot too.

Maybe you could stand in your kitchen telling your grownup about Saturn's rings.

Or sit on your bed talking to a poster about the stars in the solar system.

Especially if it's an awesome poster!
       -Jelani

When you practice, you'll learn how you communicate.

Because practicing might help you notice that you

talk fast,

sway back and forth,

tap your foot,

or want to read (all) your words from a notecard.

These are all good things to recognize so you can **work on them**.

Like, if you talk fast, your friends might not hear all the great stuff you want to share!

I struggle with talking fast. It's so hard to slow down!

- Amy

Or, if you sway, they may get distracted watching you instead of listening to you!

And, if you read all your words from a notecard, they may feel like you're talking at them, not with them.

Practice makes permanent.

-Cathey

When we speak, we want people

to listen
ideas an

to our
d stories.

Why?

Because ideas are interesting and helpful!

They can even change the world!

So, how can you become a better speaker so people will want to listen?

We have 3 ideas for you.

One. Talk to 1 person at a time.

Talk to them like you're talking with a friend.

Look them in the eye so they feel connected to you when you speak.

And then move on to another person and do the same.

Eye contact is one of the best ways to look confident in front of a group of people!

-Amy

Two. Speak clearly.

That might mean speaking more slowly or loudly.

Remember, people want to hear your ideas!

Your voice is your energy!
-Cathey

Three. Talk with passion.

Don't be afraid to gesture with your hands.

Sound excited in your voice.

Believe in what you're saying.

If you look and sound like you care about your ideas, your listeners will care too!

You've got this!

It may feel awkward
or even scary, **but be yourself**!

Practice your ideas
out loud,
a lot.

Connect with the
people listening to you.

And remember...

You have someth say and your

ing important to ideas matter.

Outro
for grownups

Now that we have shared how to develop fundamental public speaking skills, our hope is that you can help the kid in your life to continue to grow in their ability to effectively communicate and drive positive change.

Whether the goal is to engage in thoughtful debate, make a career as a motivational speaker, or gain confidence in front of an audience, public speaking can help kids achieve their dreams. This book is just the first step in that journey.

One of the often unexpected delights of public speaking is how it builds confidence. Encourage your kid to speak boldly and often about what they're passionate about, and guide them in using that passion to spark change. Let's work together to unlock our kids' potential through the power of communicating with our words!

About TED^X Portland

TEDxPortland produces experiences to create space for people to come together to spark deep discussion and connection. Established in 1984, TED stands for Technology, Entertainment, Design, and "TED Talks" explore these 3 subject areas that collectively shape our world. In 2009, TEDx was established, with "x" referring to an independently organized TED event. Portland was an early adopter, with a license to organize a local event showcasing ordinary speakers with extraordinary ideas.

About Our Contributors

Greg Bell (he/him)
Watch his **TED**^{X} Talk
Water the Bamboo

Cathey Armillas (she/her)
Speaker/Story Coach
Watch her **TED**^{X} Talk
Share Your Life

Stephen Green (he/him)
Watch his **TED**^{X} Talk
Cheat More

David Rae (he/him)
Curator **TED**^{X}Portland

Amy Wolff (she/her)
Speaker Coach
Watch her **TED**^{X} Talk
Don't Give Up: Claiming Your Personal Agency

Jelani Memory (he/him)
Watch his **TED**^{X} Talk
Kids Are Ready

Made to empower.